I

Poetry and Beauty

*

an essay

*

Traumear

Paperback ISBN 978-0-244-03804-5

*

www.traumear.com

*

By means of this essay we discover some of the ways in which effective beauty can be harnessed as poetry and how that poetry, in turn, works distinct benefits for us. The ambition is not to write 'beautiful poetry'.

iv

Poetry and Beauty

'What we know of beauty would fit on the head of a pin', someone recently told me, a student of micro-surgery at the local university and as so often happens, one forgets the face but the words remain, bothersome in the way they repeatedly crop up, as though supported by some significance – probably intensely personal.

Anyone on the lookout for beauty in poetry may find himself in the position of the traveller who can cross the chasm by the rope bridge only if he leaves all his baggage behind. If he cares more for the baggage he settles down on this side and contents himself with the view. But if he crosses he finds that he would have had no need for that baggage anyway; its comparative value was trivial.

Beauty has many names, but none of them give it completely. This fact alone makes beauty attractive. Then we should ask: Once attracted, how do we fare? Or do we fare at all? Are we moved? By way of static sensations of beauty we are taught to reach out, not to maintain but to acquire, and this acquisitive instinct has troubled many a servant in the absence of his master. What we acquire often leaves us little room for living, even for existing, and we cast about for some bedrock, on which to build a sound structure, dedicated not to beauty as she seems, perhaps a sexual phenomenon framed for a purpose, but certainly to the effects of beauty, since beauty is the sun-total of all effects.

All that we speak, in mind or tongue,
reaped by the heart from world in song,
or dared by the unspeakable in life:
small mind with a brain on fire –

leaves, as a track on sand or snow,
the tell-tale sign of joy or woe
stamped on the works by hand erected
as monuments to the passage of time.

Therefore, if an eager mood transcends
one time the bounds of narrowed flesh
and arrests in spirit a kindred soul,
fair warmed by striving towards that goal,

we may lose patience if we observe
what hindrances these two surmount,
leagued each to one, like sea to shore,
not trapped by self-love any more.

*

Now where can we look for beauty, and where can we expect it to germinate, and will we recognize it when it suddenly stands in front of us for a moment and affords us the opportunity to become familiar? Or is this way of talking about it sensible in the first place?

Personally I have been brought up to believe that beauty has an enemy, not ugliness but the philistine. This philistine, a mythological figure at the best of times if I recall correctly, demonstrates his attitudes sooner or later on all walks of life, and I was educated to recognize him, to point to him, along with my like-minded, similarly educated acquaintances, and then to dismiss him, as too far beneath contempt to merit a second notice. As the mythological figure that he was, he naturally took on, during those moments, the shape of individual people, the personality of distinct human beings, and one had to be careful, I suppose, to dismiss the myth, the bathwater, while retaining the person, the baby. I am ashamed to recall how often during my youth I failed to make that distinction as clearly as I might have done.

Not that one was taught to hate the sin and love the sinner but rather to hate the philistine and love beauty. To some degree, of course, sin and the philistine overlapped, as functioning concepts. There were, also, sins other than the ignorance of beauty, though I doubt we were cautioned to expect any that were greater. Murder, adultery, cupidity, these were judged more or less as aberrations of body or mind, poor health, physical or mental; mistakes, basically, requiring no forgiveness but excuse. A fair minded individual, so far as my own early enlightenment stretched, made it his duty to advocate the building of hospitals, prisons, and asylums in sufficient number to be able to respond to such types of deviation from the norm – those unfortunate enough to be poor deserved public charity – but he made it his policy, based on creed, to despair of the philistine, because for him there was no hope. He hated beauty and beauty was God.

I think I was brought up to prefer angels to men. Whatever the case, it did me little good. Probably it harmed me. I became suspicious of Beauty. It didn't give me room to breathe. I often preferred stupid people to the zealous disciples of Beauty, because stupid people, what little thinking they did, were at least allowed to think for

3

themselves. No golden image glowered over them, bullying them into adoration.

I dare say in my attempt to emulate my elders I indulged in a bit of bullying myself from time to time. I don't recall anyone ever coming down from the mountain to discipline and excommunicate any votaries of the golden calf. Unless … no. That was different.

*

1. The contemplation of beauty and sense perception

As soon as we trust our senses, they stop leading us, or misleading us, and they serve us. Their most suitable occupation, the one they lend themselves to most readily, is the contemplation of beauty. The task our senses are most reluctant to perform involves them in reflection and this is so because reflection is the inalienable contribution of our mind, not as it by-passes the senses but as it makes use of the trusted senses' contribution, which we call sense perception.

The contemplation of beauty is the same as sense perception: the same thing is seen here or regarded there.

If the mind attempts to reflect what the senses have not as yet fully perceived, it commits an act of bad faith. If it insists on interfering with the contemplation of beauty by the senses, it makes itself suspect and indulges in acts of viciousness. In the interest of mental soundness, therefore, we do well to practice the contemplation of beauty and to make a habit of it, so that our mind will not even be tempted to reflect prematurely.

One way to practice the **contemplation of beauty** to the point of good habit is poetry and we intend to give some examples of it:

> That the surface of table and lamp
> is light, not what we perceive
> beneath an illusion,
> the mad will's intrusion,
>
> may spark off a terror where
> all simple modulation fails.
> The fine sense quails
> before the mind's cruel eye.
>
> Reluctantly some passer-by
> folds up the scenery
> and charms the air,
> mindful of other days and ways,
>
> proud choices made,
> weak fortunes foretold.
> The classical array of lights
> managed by the horizon's round,
>
> courtesy of a night sky
> improperly festive in the past,
> could work or create
> magnificence where none exists.
>
> But the child's wise eye
> makes languish or discounts
> contrary evidence of the sage
> and its gaze would pierce every age.

*

Or sense perception:

Strong men live the life they will
while their wives are on the pill;
little children tend the garden:
life is prisoner and warden.

Anti-climax, bankrupt dreamers,
visions by belated schemers;
fellows at the College Ball:
Bless us, lord, we know them all.

Calcium for the teeth and bones,
robots copulate with drones;
larval stage on road to lightning:
earth grows fruitful, sky is brightening.

Magic of the sort that loses,
coward's heart that self-abuses;
intellect that walks on air:
candidate for the electric chair.

Prophylactic mind on ice,
hand on holster once or twice;
art exhibit city centre:
silently the moon-men enter.

Fog lies thick on marsh and crater,
life declines, but that comes later;
fork in road, eclipse of sun:
truth makes hearts stop, love moves none.

*

2. The generation of beauty

The contemplation of beauty and sense perception are the same. Beauty does not have an effect but it is the sum total of all effects, and this may be registered in terms of poetry, so that words become both burden and carrier. Each and every word has magnitude, on account of being a word, and it has dimension, which means that whether spoken or heard, its capacity to move is absolute.

Usually we think of beauty as a state of being or as a capacity to delight, to enchant and so on. However as human beings we ourselves are capable of beauty, of generating beauty on a scale that surpasses any form or fashion of life. Our capacity for beauty has to be recognized as fundamental to our desire for beauty, so that capacity and desire for it readily interchange and become one.

The generation of beauty is not everybody's business and of course neither does it have to be. Some are picked for it and a few are chosen, so let no one quarrel with the gifts he possesses by comparing them vainly to those of another. Of course we may ask for more.

It seems that in order to generate beauty a certain willingness is required to hold out, initially, before a storm of internal inquiries as to the suitability of one's organism for the task, and while it remains difficult, if not impossible, to ascertain the origin of these inquiries, one soon learns the necessity of responding to them in a definite and forthright manner, if one intends to respond at all rather than simply side-stepping the issue, which can be done with not much more than minimal and momentary loss of face.

The definite and forthright response however, if protracted and sustained over a period of time, gains for us a powerful skill, which is the skill to invest beauty with love, and it is love that lends beauty it's power. Without love, beauty has not power but might. Mighty beauty may stun us, overwhelm us, shock our sensibility but it cannot be of use to us as human beings. The best we can do is pretend how it might suit us, if ... but it cannot in fact. So we do a clever thing when we familiarize ourselves thoroughly with the occurrence of this so-called 'pure' beauty, and with the uncanny craving and lust for it that has ruined many a worthy person.

The quality of character required to withstand the might of beauty is sexual strength, which is strength specifically male or female, and the quality of character that is needed if we are not to react to it is chastity, which is sexual energy sustained in the face of the asexual.

The investment of beauty with love, however, is a case of its might not being contested but transformed into a power, and this transformation of might into power, in the aspect of beauty, is what we mean by the generation of it.

The poetic generation of beauty proceeds like this, for example:

> I cannot alter the ways of the world,
> trapped within love, and love is hurled
> within me, through popular confusion,
> where all the fair folk stand, awaiting
> the high wire act, celebrating

ahead of time angelic forces
that would, like stars, except for mercy
and the law that sleeps in weight of stone,
improvise grand Saviour tactics,
bring superman within our sphere

and claw the eyes from dead men's faces.
What I can do is unexpected and moves
with caution along busy thoroughfares,
not brilliant where the time's sickness needs
quiet consoling, or the night light,

but hopeful when the factories shut,
clement to counter too much purity
where little ones starve, right emaciated,
quick to apply the gift that here
surrounds our spiritual atmosphere.

Please fold me too in stronger arms,
for the merging of lands within
makes nations seem so spiteful poor,
there, in ideal circumstance, where the globe
means our garden, fenced by shape,

a clever provision, if you take my point,
and not to be ignored much longer.
Of course we always suppose
that as our own intelligence grows
so ought the persons' in high places.

This only testifies to dreams we leave
or sleep we lose, not taste for facts
that should dictate the mastered self,
the fool suffered gladly, with a laugh
and an eye secretly on the histograph.

The tissue we call history of mankind,
god's gown grown manifold diverse,
suited to satisfy our thirst for time,
surrounds each moment of each day
and fashions itself images of men.

*

3. The description of beauty

The experience of beauty involves justice. If it is justice we want, and if we thirst for justice, the experience of beauty will fill our need.

For the very first description of beauty we need look no further than the environment of our eye, of our organ of sight. Whatever pertains to that environment participates in beauty.

All the various details of which the eye's environment is made up cannot help but entail beauty. Therefore we need only to name them and the justice of their connection will be revealed.

What we look at and what we see is not necessarily the same and consequently we should remain aware of which of these we do, because the difference between the two is liable to lead us astray, so that we may mistake our eye's environment for our own, which it decidedly is not. Watch, therefore, that this does not happen.

The eye surrounds itself with light
and straightaway the sun shines through.
Its rays illuminate our sight
with shades of yellow, red and blue.

10

The purple hills, examined well,
distribute cloud within their sphere
and leisurely the rivers fell
where trees and meadowland appear.

*

What we look at and see, the looking and the seeing,
more particularly, helps to unite what appears to be outside of us with what appears to be within, and so it heals.
The environment of our eye, again, is moulded from a
single sphere, not either outside or inside of us, not without nor within, but always both, or of both. The beauty of
this appeals to our eye, and so we trust it to do the work
for which it was created:

By the moon's eternal light
the sea leaps high
and the smouldering rock
kisses the wave
and the wave leaps back,
takes time to ascend

far north once more,
adhering to the special ice,
and the temperate light
leaves the flesh satisfied.

*

To trust our eye to do its work and to watch whether
it looks or sees, not to use it as a tool or as an instrument,
as we do our eyes, this is what makes the difference. The
blindness that comes with insisting on only the outer eyes
or, for that matter, on only the inner eye, sometimes

called the mind's eye, can become so ingrained that we make it a point of pride and honour, of our intellectual integrity, no less. So we may say in all honesty, that beauty can persuade us to drop our blindness, habitual or partial, and in every sense of the word – to open our eyes:

> The fox disturbs the nestling swan
> and oh, the willows dream consent,
> while overhead, in feathery white,
> the female fears its force is spent
>
> but plunges through the darkling sky,
> immoderate for the fox's throat,
> too late to stop the killing beast,
> though not the deed it would promote.

If it happens that our eye feels pain, due most probably to the unaccustomed nature of the activity, to its freedom, we need only remember, for the sake of its ease, that what we see is not separate or divorced from the act of seeing, and that our eye may well be reclaiming some territory here, lost in the past due to the mind's error, acquired or inherited.

As the strength of our eye increases, so does the depth and extent of its environment. Our description of that environment becomes more masterful and a greater degree of beauty is entailed, by the poetry, remember, not by the poem. The poem in question, or under scrutiny, has nothing to do with beauty. Poetry is the wine : the poem is the glass.

Once again we encourage our eye to look and to see, for the sake of a description of its environment, and we watch, so that we do not confuse our own environment

with that of our eye. The independence of our eye guar-
antees the self-evidence of its environment, which in turn
implies the ready availability of beauty pure and simple:

So narrow the valley,
so deep, pitched steep,
and the river foaming below there,
creating the rainbowed mixture of mist and air,

and we, steadied perhaps on the wooden bridge,
blossoms of cherry laurel far and wide
of a whiteness nearly possible to describe
but matched by the giant hogweed's umbel of light,

we question, and patiently stare,
spelled by the rush, the roar of lit air.
Our courtesy must,
built by design,
lie in wait in the trembling clime.

And lo and behold,
the woods open, the brown mare proceeds,
thumping the turf, the forest floor nearly hollow.
A foal and a stallion follow,
black bear in pursuit.

The holly tree stands in the open field
with crimson berries it would yield,
torn from dark branches by the bear,
the glistening leaves, their tissue fair
ripped by the careless brute –
but of no interest to the mare.

The foal, now safe,
drinks from the stream,
but frightened, leaps aside,

the canny nostrils testing for the scent,
blond flanks combed by the wind,
thistle-down catching in the mane.

In the brook the trout
responds to the dull thud,
the clug of stone rolled against stone
set off by the stallion's hoof.

The static bridge still makes no sound
but the wasteful eyes of the observer there
gulp in the blue of intermittent air.
Some leaves fall from the vast beech bough.

*

4. The contemplation of reflected beauty

After the first description of beauty, in the eye's environment, we pass on to the contemplation of reflected beauty, not as it corresponds to some system of thought but as it surpasses all such thought and unites itself with reason.

The role that reason plays during the generation of beauty is peripheral and during the description of beauty reason allocates the activity of the heart, when we watch to keep the environment of the eye discrete. However the discrepancy between our own environment and that of the eye must be made up, and this is where reason comes in. It supports the eye as it develops its functions and supplies us with guidelines as the poetry proceeds.

Reason has its own grounds for existence. Without reason we can do nothing and be nothing but with reason, or in reason, we can be and do what we wish. It depends entirely on us, therefore, whether we insist on seeing merely the difference between things or whether we see reason. Because to see reason is no empty phrase. When we do it we have ourselves entirely in our power.

The way to deal with reasons, of course, is by way of thought, just as the way to deal with beauty is by way of appearances. However appearances in isolation, as in the case of mechanical constructs or accidental sensations, have no use and are worthless, while thought to no end, perpetrated merely on account of appearances, cannot have any value but it dissipates and destroys.

We are faced therefore with the task of bending our thought to some reasonable purpose and of revealing appearances in beauty. This may be accomplished in exemplary fashion with the help of poetry. And, more specifically to the present point, we may bend our thought to the purpose of revealing appearances, in beauty, even as we choose to reveal those appearances which stem from, and are due to, our thought. In this way reason and beauty are brought together and made one, or allowed to become one, or shown to be one:

> The sails of our tradition have been filled
> by much that came there only due to folly,
> but how it moved! The whirlwind of self-willed
> amusement caused by ivy twined around holly
>
> was reaped, as one was erstwhile led to expect,
> by poor men not of valour but heroic
> in terms of right. Their high minds still infect
> the flesh of babes. We may not like their stoic

15

reliance on the death of brain and heart,
their flourishes in front of mobs and masses
of what we feel, but spellbound in our art
we reap no sense, while cynic's bark outclasses

man's word, that may be live and filled to bursting
with real food for the hungry and the thirsting.

*

Caught unaware where the water
tumbles over the cliff's brow
and the sun's hard ray glances
off the line where sky meets water

the eye reaches beyond itself
and projects for the earth an illumination.

We clearly define,
if we choose carefully betimes,
the blossom afloat on the
pond's still surface,

therefore by all means available
retain the gratitude of the eye.

By the time night falls
and people have gone where people
tend to go when night falls,
to various submarine places –

listen how the storm howls!
it frightens me – by this time I draw

the consoling garment of the spirit
close around me, forward stepping
and outward in trust striding
in his company who surely knows;

whose milk white steed steps
high to its knees in sagacity.

It crosses the stream where the
pine's roots reach beneath the stream bed,
wickedness left behind to the brave,
ahead free wisdom of darlings –

ahead too, and within now, my pet,
ample trout glistening in the shallows.

Those who know what this means
should not speak out, but hide
their knowledge under the heart's stone,
there to learn gravity and time's trial –

or else keep quiet out of courtesy
and let happiness bear fruit for others.

Under a star-studded sky
a dry hot wind still parches the land,
much to my consternation, and I retreat,
I cautiously seek shelter from this

dry hot wind that sticks
the tongue to the roof of the mouth.

Sleep has much to recommend it,
at this or any other round hour,
but one sleep I would not care to revisit,
where Snow White lies behind the
                              twentieth century

17

and no sweet prince cometh,
for the lack of belief's wakeful seed.

So I cherish the memory of the bright cloud
projected outward as into a still-life,
where even the light is hard and sound
and bodies cannot interfere with one another

because all vanity is taken up immediately
by the next full gesture, claimed

perhaps as original home by none other
than owner who open-handed owns
and cares with a royal care
not only while the conscience watches.

*

The gentle mind, given to play,
to leisure near the border of the rose garden,
notices the anguish of the child
and must, if life is to continue,

draw on the assurance of the distant hills,
pale ghosts of hills, since veiled
against the eye's impatient penetration.

   In those hills the white birds nest
and they approach in large-winged flight,
swooping and meandering, settling nowhere,
ever promising, sweetly foretelling,
voluptuous truths, luxurious rest.

Kind eyes of unkind birds, you search
in me for bearings to your existence.
Thoughts home-made and home-making give
man's spirit eventually cause to live.

18

You messengers from origin in hills,
where tribal men drown in habitual sleep,
must share the responsibility for the contagion,
the sickness centred in endless time taken,
ill health bred on towards a timeless end
and gladly I spill your tireless blood.

Oh now, how roars the storm, sure, make it
less of a sensation, this death of yours:
I too hear the crunch of the heel on gravel
or sip excitement from a moment's lips, only
not such bombast, dear denizens of the air,
such mighty flappings, squirting of blood,
spray of blood foam to good effect on wing.
Such terror and trembling due to a beheading!

One would think nations had not engulfed the globe
nor violets suffered the factory's encroachment.

But of course they have, and faultless people roam
near these tenements, desperate for fire.
They crane their necks, the rose garden eludes them,
the white birds never die under their knives.

*

The contemplation of reflected beauty, given in the three examples, denies us nothing but affords us a benign insight into the workings of the mind, where we come to terms with reflected beauty. The terms themselves are physical, which means that they imply both body and mind, and consequently the justice inherent in beauty is presented unavoidably, but of course in an impartial manner. Whichever way of approach we adopt, we cannot encroach, to our detriment, on any alleged source or origin of beauty, while the effects of beauty as such are eased into our consciousness; eased, fundamentally, due to automatic persuasion by reason.

Only while reason is allowed to operate automatically, rather than being systematically constrained, morally restrained, or stupidly just plain strained, can it take on those particular shapes and forms of thought that correspond exactly and apply eminently to the available measures of beauty. Paragons of beauty, like models of reason, generally have use only to the extent that they make possible the virtues of experiment, and these virtues are then only fruitful in turn.

So just in passing, we may describe a paragon of beauty as the sum-total of all experimental effects, and we may define a model of reason as a system of perfect thought.

*

5. Experience of beauty and intuitive poetry

How we go about making our references to whatever experience of beauty we have undergone, or are presently undergoing, depends to a large extent on our willingness, if not readiness, to be moved by beauty. So first of all we ought to be able to recognize the various introductions to such experience, and here we apply the simple test of intuition. Anyone is capable of intuition, we only have to learn how to call on it at a moment's notice and how to bring it most immediately into effect.

Because on intuition depends – and intuition is what we call – the perfect ease of our being while under the influence of external effects and since beauty is always at least to some degree something else altogether, the externality of such effects is guaranteed and we may take the ease under their influence for granted.

Perfect ease while under the influence of external effects is intuitive: that way of putting it is bound to be instructive. There is the ease we feel and the ease we know, while both are bound up intuitively in perfection. Contrary and opposed to this perfection we find all the various states of poor health that may plague us from time to time, and these would urge us to make significant contributions by way of intuitive knowledge and understanding. So a correct introduction, not to say: an expedient one, to the experience of beauty is not neither here nor there, but both here and there. A highly developed power of intuition is tantamount to the act of healing. Intuitive poetry trains us towards that, and in that development, first by aiding us in the recognition of the effects alluded to, sharpening our wits with respect to them, and then by gaining for us, little by little, as we take on what one might call rather appropriately the trusteeship, the capacity to give forceful expression to our intuitive powers:

> Go on, make the green heights ring
> with joyous voices, the low land sink
> into seasonal oblivion, then to rise
> once again fruitful.

> Bring love to bear on winter's things,
> fling off the dirge detrimental, wrap
> in birch bark moistened in oil
> the feverish feet.

Climb less avidly now towards
the world's wisdom to draw the sting,
question the self-leavening lustre
as flashed forth from bellies of
birds on wing.

Do not decline the challenge
thrown out by aches and pains,
even the trivia of an existence made
drab by the lack of illusion,
too much delusion.

Recall the pursed lips on a
summer's day, when the heat reddened
even the atmosphere beneath the bridge
and eagle eyes stared.

*

I made no pronouncements
but spare the word them who would
spare me the sight of themselves, as though
her imperial majesty the queen could
dictate all fairyland.

We make the mountains tremble
with our henchmen hired for food and
clothing, our lip service paid to
uncles and aunts of the diseased
remnants of humanity.

Go on and heighten
the colour in your cheek, young Miss,
to catch your stallion, why not,
live and let live, ask for the moon,
take tigers to bed with you and
bask in the limelight.

This has me wondering, because
the problems we cut off trees like
nerves from the brainstem, to
ripen in the bag on our back, life's
cross, how can we make them
suit our situation?

Do we not all hold hands with
the god who makes us, can we not
prefer the tissues of enlightenment as it
mends, to safeguard us against
the wilful intrusion?

The rich man, educated
beyond the powers of his consumption,
looks askance at the wool trader's lot,
climbs naked and freezing behind the
bulwarks of intellect, hides in the last
ditch of his desire.

We make no comment but mend
our own ways hopefully, not content with
eager assurances of love and care
by the local council, but neither despicable,
discountenanced by the void left
by the political heroes.

We sing nevertheless, on account,
and the sad tale of events foisted
by newspapers and television on our kin
is lowered by endless rope down
into a bottomless pit, the rope cut,
there, it's gone now.

Certainly I could make accusations,
and who can say but they'd stick
smack against my own soul, this abused
bird of paradise, neglected so long
by stingy vegetarians it thought its
throat had been cut.

*

Intuitive poetry may not be to our taste but the question of taste should not be allowed to arise in its case. Technically speaking, this poetry must seem objectionable, even ludicrous, while not in use, or while misapplied. One should not allow oneself to develop a distaste for it, however. Sickness and illness, all forms of disease mental or physical, are bound to initiate an antipathetic reaction in the so-called healthy organism, for a similar reason. If we have our wits about us, however, we do not allow ourselves to judge according to this organism, but we override its reactions responsibly in terms of, and in the interest of, wellbeing. [1]

Now this sounds as though I were comparing intuitive poetry to an unhealthy organism; I certainly don't mean that. The misunderstanding can only arise where

---

[1] See the author's book: A New Look at Wellbeing and Health, pg. 19, re: organism and wellbeing.

one forgets that poetry not in application is not poetry at all, but sport for the unwary, a pastime for the unaware.

As we do gradually enter the realm of our inner feeling now, of what we rather remarkably choose to call our emotional life, the areas of passion and compassion, of sympathy, empathy and pathos, literary or otherwise, we could do worse than submit to a short refresher course on how we would like to see these various concepts used. In my own personal case I do differentiate rather carefully between what I would like to value and what not; which areas I would prefer to see opened to further research and where precisely I should like to draw the line, either permanently or only for the time being, until prudence suggests progress.

6. The effects of beauty on our organism; subtle energy

So it does come to me as a bit of a shock when I realize how sparsely documented is my own conviction with respect to such questions as the effect of beauty, or its potential influence, on, say, a callous heart; on insensibility due to starvation of the intellect; on various ingrained habits of rotten enthusiasm, laziness of the emotions and their stimulants, downright unwillingness to undergo hurtful sensations due to nothing more than a bad record in the past. How, for example, can the specific incursions of experimental justice due to beauty, as experience or otherwise, reclaim some of the territory razed by prolonged provocation due to cynicism, embitterment due to sarcasm, treachery due to a gleeful ruthlessness – whatever the excuses or justifications for these, if any?

25

Due to our various poetic intuitive excursions into the realm of the unknown we have acquired both a sensibility for the openness of our organism to instruction and a sensitivity to the various rejection symptoms and reaction phenomena that we can expect from ourselves, under trial or just plain as exposed to trickery.

As soon as the human organism, as compared to the human being, is required to undergo something, it must react, and we should not ask it or expect it to do different. Our organic make-up cannot be depended upon to subscribe to alteration of its state: by definition the organism is static. It strives by its nature to maintain its static condition. There are logical reasons for this. For one, it makes organic activity scientifically predictable to the human mind. The popular mind cannot come to any recognizable terms with this, but it need not concern us here. Predictable organic activity cannot over- whelm us, like that aspect of beauty we touched on earlier, but it supplies us with the sort of energy that allows us to cope.

For every challenge presented to the human organism, a supply of **subtle energy** is made available, given a suitable, appropriate and sufficient degree of scientific [1] prediction. In the absence of such prediction, organic activity is wasteful, self-destructive or strange.

Subtle energy is not particular, but it has peculiar characteristics, and these we must learn to identify, because where- and whenever emotions amount to more than 'copyistic indiscriminations' – animal warmth –

---

[1] By 'scientific' I mean: intending to contribute to the understanding of something.

they involve subtle energy; and where our passions are based more soundly than a popular image can maintain – repetitive histrionics – they reside in subtle energy; and when our well-being is more than an abundance of high spirits and felt vitality – good health – it promotes subtle energy, and so tends to become permanent.

The human organism is eventually challenged or under control. It either must exist, within the confines of our own existence, or else it may exist, under the controlled conditions of art, and this the latter possibility is much to be preferred. The challenge we offer our organism, in terms of poetry, say, allows us to dictate our own terms and to work them out in freedom.

The eventual challenge, which is to say: the challenge by events and due to events, compares to the controlled challenge mainly in that it necessitates pain, whereas the latter presumes suffering. The presumption of suffering makes pain unnecessary.

What interests us here, consequently, is how we should go about poetry in order to challenge our organism in a controlled fashion, so that we may suffer its predictable reactions to our challenge and thereby make subtle energy available and accessible to ourselves. Remember that the eventual challenge is a case not only of something happening to us, nor yet in addition to this of our noticing, due to pain, that something has happened to us, but even further, of our accepting pain in general not as something merely to be got rid of as soon as possible each and every time – although one certainly isn't suggesting it should be prolonged, dear heavens! – but, dare we say it: as an interpretative function of an organic reluctance to change. The pain tells us that our organism refuses to change and that somehow it must have been asked to do so. Of course we can refuse utterly to regard this as a challenge, and we can equally choose to consider every pain, physical, emotional or mental, as accidental interference, by alien condition, circumstance or environment, with our presumed steady state of life. Personally I prefer to allocate the presumption elsewhere.

The only other point to be made, for the argument to be complete, has to do with the value of subtle energy as such. What good is it?

Once we fully understand the nature of our situation as human beings on the earth for a time, the question sounds as absurd as the answer must seem ridiculous, since it falls into the same category with: Why should we enjoy pleasure when instead we could be in pain? But pleasure has been made so suspect, and suffering so morbid, by the dead, that only a few ever seem to come up with the courage to look at the matter afresh and with the circumspection that is advisable.

The continued rejection of this subtle energy, therefore, specifically leads to chronic states of one sort or another, and it is the rejection itself which causes the chronic state. The materialist vainly hopes to remain aloof, neither to eat nor to have pangs of hunger, and of course his success may be measured precisely by the degree of his desolation and the extent of his fixity. – My own regrettable materialist misconceptions usually hinge on some confusion of perfection and simplicity with completeness and finish.

Health appertains to an organism, not to a being, and a healthy organism is one that produces subtle energy. A human being therefore cannot be understood to be healthy, any more than an organism can be said to be well. But if an organism ceases to produce subtle energy it 'diseases'.

One might do well to remind of the relationship of individuality, being and humanity here too, in passing. The human being is not individual, nor is a human being an individual, but it has individuality, and individuality can at this stage of the proceedings be understood as the nature of our organism. It is the nature of our organism to remain individual. Its organic state as such is not natural but habit. The good habit of our organism accrues to it, by dint of its production of subtle energy; it does not arrive with it at birth.

Organic beings are self-contradictory, while human organisms are pleonastic. We have to keep on eye on the language we use or else soon we have nothing to talk about; on account of not having spoken well, that sort of thing.

Our other, and related, concept, that of presumed suffering – not presumptuous suffering – allows us to cope now with the role of art, of poetry in particular, as a challenge to the organism. Due to this concept we may bring just beauty to bear on our organism with the result of subtle energy in our human being:

Nowhere do we reckon so well,
so finely with the trembling heart,
　　as here, backed against this wall.

England, your precious mother tongue,
　　so suited to the careful rule,
helps me to protect and to prolong

　　my genius, prostrate beneath this sun.
Such heat requires much reckoning.
　　Such light has turned my gaze again

and my eye, once lost to love out there,
　　put out by stars and sun and moon,
returns now to perception clear,

　　to strange sights within the garden.
We do not know love any more.
　　Our stiff necks will not bend for burden

nor may a summer's day goad
　　to mirth our shades before they shorten,
our moods while the sun's rays wait.

　　Yet we may give fair report,
while the lamb's conquests abide,
　　according to the lights of our art.

*

A wagon creaks across the plains.

We see this with experienced eye
but turn away, to hide our shame.

The frozen mountains in the west,
the strife and hatred in the east,
these darken like a cloud our brow.

What song will cheer the weeping women
huddled around the campfire there,
bewailing the slaughter of their men
by natural cause or hand of fate?

I have not depth nor strength of heart
to comprehend man's suffering
nor his elation when he dies,
tried by prescriptions from his mind,
by contempt for his flesh convicted.

If all it takes is to reach out
and pluck the fruit by history bred
with ease, not earned nor gained by self,
why do we make hardship our friend
and cling to him as though he could save
us from our blindness and our woe?

If we were where we are meant to be
and our image of our finished state
were coincident with our environment,
not monstrous the one, so that the other might
affect repair, in subservience,
the abyss of death perpetuated
half by the unwillingness to concede
the victory where it does most good

half by insistence on comparison
of present man with forms of life
as though the crown that graced the head
held pre-eminence over what it crowned –

we would be entitled to all this:

First, garment of things visible
to keep the sensuous body clothed,
that wind and rain and heat and frost
should seem like playthings of the mind,
not harbingers of a corruption
beneath contempt, goads to survival,
else not even blood and breath should flow
gladly, but one stifle the other.

Then happy acceptance of all gifts
vouchsafed by one who exists again
not still, tied to god's apron strings.
These are the gifts our desire requires:

Sensuous control of all things past,
accompaniments to life on earth
in present day, by light fulfilled
and an acute awareness of
simple delights that grow each day
and demonstrate, without reproach,
time's haphazard prodigality
wedded to no uncertain hope

nor given to trespass as we go;
some inkling of diurnal snow
and, child! we fetch the pine trees in
as though our life began at birth.

Let genius speak: it understands.

No more sleep, eyes fixed on dreams,
but darkness of the sort that holds
itself in check, light's common fold
of rich, black velvet for our heads
to rest on, as we drift in sleep
in like direction as we walk
through wakeful hours, not down in mouth
and spirits, but down in gravity.

Here the ground is well prepared,
for planting, building, digging wells,
for imagining how land and sea
give life-support to please the gods.

The final state of our affairs
is finished when no harm exists
to sway us from our chosen task
and we prefer the thing we love.

That we may choose and not be shocked,
may play perfection's game at will
just as eternal life moves on
in us, and we in it, my friends,
my live friends, borne in heaven-on-earth
or how you call it, and whether or no;
that all these things have come to pass
and once being past, give generous aid:

one man makes his determined care.

The sky's reflection in the stream
holds steady while the waters move
and spring, with all its many terrors,
lies brimming where the meadow blooms.

Search for enchanted isles in mind
by all means to exploit your youth
but when the teeth of hard luck grip
and tear your magic by the throat,
be it humanist or materialist
or piously offered up to saints,
reach for this memory where it crops
and boldly call it reality.

All that is world has final time
and none may obliterate its track
or change to horse power power of man
to trace his origin and come back.

We who have settled here and live
in god's own time, at god's own will,
not willing to dispute our cause
or entertain the urge to kill,

give notice now of our intent
to tremble when the knife makes room
for silence bound to edge of sound
made by the shapes our lips assume,

while tranquil hands caress plain face
to urge necessity of trust
and sometimes teach beyond love's reach
to show how love can be unjust,

except it move in beauty's sphere,
not trapped, nor by its eye ensnared,
but freely leading, freely led,
not by the nose, while skin is bared.

Such thoughts as these make time worthwhile
and speedy resurrection – claim
for creature great and creature small
united in one common name.

* *

I was so unhappy in those days
before I learned to trust these words
to lead me back. – Why back?

Say rather: evolution, by way of
Plato, Schopenhauer, then Schubert
experimenting on liquid keyboards.

But you moved in and out of arms,
never satisfied, only dimly aware of
some reason why you had been born.

Forget all that. Look at the snow now
lightly on our eyelashes, a cool morning,
Schubert giving shape to the silence.

You don't realize the importance of the role of
fantasy in your life. Will it stir the heart,
can it help you eat that delicious sunrise?
Snow melts, crystal drops plummet –

Well, I make it a condition of my life.
It helps me stay ahead of what would otherwise
lie itself into my life, as though it existed.
Something evil would create itself out of nothing.

Aha, I see! You should get out more.
Expose your stale emotions to the fresh air,
to the scent of winter heliotrope, to the
plunging of waves against rock at the shore.

I carry these sensations of failure and success,
of boredom and fear, around with me,
of bliss, your actual absolute happiness,
because I expect them to bear fruit in me.
I do take appearances rather seriously.
Some have accused me of wishful thinking.

I hope you thank them for it, in good voice.

The one I trust most readily just tells me
to get out of his way, let him get on with it,
and for a naturally active person like myself
that's a full time occupation. I call it
developing my natural resources. But sometimes
I can't turn the pain down like the sound on
the radio, and then I panic, slightly.

Everyone does that. It happens to everyone.

Good. Or rather: I am sorry. But then
why do you tell me that? You must have a
reason for telling me that. Do you charge me
with self-indulgence? Or do you react to my
aesthetic challenge of your complacency?
I can leave you alone entirely if you like.
Would you prefer it if I turned away? Let me
offer you the therapy of the metaphor.

Alright, don't worry, you haven't silenced me.
I need time to reflect. Your irritating manner
of suffocating me, of the time for reflection,
has to be suffered by someone. I do it gladly
but it irritates me all the same: This need for
somebody's feelings to sacrifice. Could you not
plant a tree of life in your own self for once?

You mean like this? Am I doing it now?
Can you stand there and watch me do it and
point to me, saying: Yes, now, that's you doing it?

Still a dependency on Aristotle, Aquinas –
then you want, for a genuine contribution
because the Arts became a National Heritage,
rivalry between composers of atomic substance,
a free-for-all pursuit of prestige as image,
spectral cataclysms encouraged by philosophers,
prancings in the limelight, stars shooting
and shot at, all equally a coward's subterfuge.
Brilliant moments setting off slack self-pity.
All this had to be reworked and revalued,
put on a new footing, the clay feet discarded.

No one knows what the future brings, because
the future brings nothing – we bring the future,
creating some of it in our likeness, so
that depends on what we choose to be; also
structuring some of it in the likeness of him
who irradiates all beauty like a crown of thorns
but meaning glorious royal gold, not blood.

Then, too, letting some of it be, which does not
happen readily, but must be induced to happen,
the inspiration of the beetle on the rose leaf.
And the clouds form into protection over us,
so please do not fear the mushroom cloud,
nor struggle to get away from the snail shape,
from the flames consuming manuscript sheets
or any other thing man-made or god-sped
because the past brings its own valid conclusion.

I taste the word, it coats my lips, shapes
their musculature to give birth to speech,
to lay the ghost of the wisdom of the sages.

Then again, this is not myself I advertise,
but you, you choose, you interrupt the score
and make amends. Above all, do live.

Do not finish prior to the time
nor complete the world's fine legend
without right away turning to the world.

You emphasize the spiral of our time
and cherish some dull moment's loquacity
but also lift the curse of race and tribe.

While any desire still masks itself as pain
you must, or may, depending on who you are
or choose to be, gratify that same desire.

Pay no heed to those who over-generalize,
mistaking the lute for the large acceptance
of all manner of thing, good or indifferent.

Work out only as much as need
dictates; there is no need to bleed.
Include the bulrush and the reed.

Fear not, you have no mouths to feed
except those mouths agape for food
contained in words and as the word.

Therefore practice no more peculiar style
nor fashion images but to last a while,
then drift and float and melt away.

Nothing that lasts is meant to stay
and the incorrigible flesh must hide
or squeak into some cold, damp corner

where death sits grinning, eager pleased
because of torment, havoc released
and the whole dumb show on record squeezed.

And that, too, must go on and on
until god's plan is done
and he has time to think up another one.

* * *

39

7. The practice of beauty; artistic influence and abstract poetry

We deal with beauty by way of appearances, as was mentioned earlier. We can think of this as appearances we make and put in ourselves. It is up to me entirely whether or not I decide to appear, and so my appearance becomes wholly a question of praxis.

The practice of beauty, or beauty in action as we may call it, begins with an insight into the effects of beauty as causes. The notion of beauty as a cause, or as a series, or chain, of causes, may not right away appeal to us, especially once we have accustomed ourselves to thinking of beauty as the sum total of all effects; but whether envisioned or seen, beauty is the same and we should let that reassure us. Constrained by the pedantry of aesthetics one naturally remains reluctant in one's responses to the preparations and protections of another ego, and while philosophy is private or public in its end, one forgets how the overriding purpose of all activity is not oblivion but more life.

The effects of beauty, that *are* beauty, may be held against the intellect so that in time they become causes. Intellectual presence, not activity, is required to cause an effect, which is to say: to turn an effect into a cause. Here we stand at the apex of artistic influence, and our criterion for saying so resides in the evidence of what we mean.

Our popular mind tends to think of effects as being caused externally within matter (materialism) in the way that a billiard ball on the move (cause) hits another billiard ball and somehow, by some inherent magic, transmits its motion to it, moving it or deflecting its motion (effect). In the wink of an eye that effect is then called a cause within a new set of circumstances, when another ball gets struck by ball number two, and so on, but this, with all due respects, ends up being no more than a lot of illustrated balls. Eventually all the world cries out for a unified field theory. If one could only find the glue!

Or else our popular imagination pictures effects as being caused internally within darkness, (determinism), where one event sparks off another to the automatic profit or loss of the latter, or else energy is conserved but then space bends! No more of that.

Turning away from this popular view of things, we can state that intellect causes effects and that intellect is the cause of effects. We do not have intellect, or an intellect, beyond this practical issue. Also, the cause of an effect is brought about intellectually and all intellectual activity is a case of effects being caused, or of causes being put to good effect. To those for whom language is a code this cannot make sense.

An isolated effect cannot be caused and must therefore first be brought into unison. Then it becomes capable of beauty. By the same token can a number of effects not be caused and they must first be united and dealt with as one. One effect lends itself to intellectual activity, as do all effects, and we come to terms with them scientifically, in order to understand them, or artistically, for the sake of joy and pleasure. One does not exclude the other. No one in his right mind would separate nourishment from the taste of food. Both exist, not to confuse the issue but for the sake of our appearance and due to it.

41

Generated beauty, as we discussed it earlier, is not essentially different from caused beauty, as we have touched on here. We distinguish between the two, however, for the sole reason of intellectual discrimination, against degenerate beauty, on the quiet, or, which it may also be called: artistic beauty.

Artistic beauty cannot be made sense of, which is a good enough reason for denying it, but in addition we sense how this beauty is degenerate because it operates against the senses and misleads to purblindness. Anyone apprehended in the act of purblindness should immediately be subjected to intensive care, before stupidity sets in and takes root. The fruits of stupidity are legion. Or we might say: They are *lesions*.

Beginning with the organ of the independent eye, here the hurtful effect of degenerate beauty is fixative. The eye is persuaded, by apparent circumstance (conditioning), to give up ordinary clear sight in order to indulge itself in a visual fixation. The antidote: abstract art.

Abstract poetry might run like this:

> Carefully locate in the brain
> the testament to illumination. Make fast
> corrections to the moon. Face
> the illusion of god's plaster cast
> and take into account
> where possible, though not of the essence:
> The human race does not amount
> to a divine excrescence.

*

42

Any active opposition to morbidity cannot help but seem absurd at times. This should not put us off and indeed it is not meant to do so. It is intended to remove even physical inhibitions from our organ of sight. Once this organ gets caught up in self-indulgence of any sort it aggravates its environment by disfiguring it. Such disfigurations must then be excised, or at least washed off, like graffiti. Pictorially assessed, abstract art scrapes off the scratches or washes off the layer through which the scratches were made. Visually self-indulgent poetry can be countenanced and counteracted from an abstract point of view. This is equally true. What we must not do is get caught up in a process of poetic, or any other, abstraction to the detriment of re-established beauty. Any curative effect can be turned into an addiction unless we mind what we do. The addiction in this case would show up as a craving for luxury, opulence, vulgarity and the like.

Abstract poetry, therefore, operates in the direction of practical achievement, and it alleviates the pathogenesis of the eye.

*

8. Censorship and didactic poetry

We call that artistic beauty where an artist tries to persuade us of his own beauty. He usually does it in a roundabout way, giving us copies and imitations of himself which he then praises, so he indoctrinates his followers with putative standards of beauty abstracted from himself or his own nature.

The proper term to describe what we do when we say no to degenerate beauty should really be censorship and I

43

have to use it for that reason because of its ultimate suitability, in spite of its routine misapplication within the sphere of our supra-civilized mentality.

Censorship is an activity of intellection insofar as we differentiate between generation and degeneration, between the desire to grow and the tendency to decline, or, viewed from the other side, between the tendency to increase and the desire to limit, where in both cases the tendency is to be deplored while the desire is to be nurtured; and it is a practical, applied exercise in taste, the sensation, an employment of tongue and nose, really, with respect to the organs we use. Finally the use we put them to in the event of censorship, (the event, not the act) distinguishes between nature and spirit, between the organic and the human, to the benefit equally of both. (Notice we don't say: between the flesh and spirit, between the animal and the human; an act of intelligence.) Thirdly, to keep censorship away from censure, from anything to do with blaming, condemnation or criticism, there must be involved an interest, and the exploration of interest, even of curiosity.

Intellection, instinct and interest go into the making of worthwhile censorship, contrary to degenerate or artistic beauty.

The interest we take in artistic activity of any sort dictates or preconditions our attitude towards what we consider to be natural and our opinion of what pertains to the flesh. (This may take some time to sort out and I hope to keep it as straightforward as possible.) Beauty, the sum-total of all effects, should not be confused with the flesh, which is the sum-total of all phenomena. To the degree that it is confused, a depravity sets in and the organization of our talents becomes corrupt.

We help ourselves out with a didactic poem:

> Censure of the mind's pure eye
> aggravates that pained expression
> tempted from reluctant granite.

> But the visual field out there,
> ploughed and harrowed, dreams to sow,
> hides the gold too – and its glow.

Didactic poetry makes use of the justice of beauty to set matters straight that would otherwise be in danger of dissipation.

> Wearily the will's pronouncements
> trudge along the path of truth,
> outraged by the eagle's screaming,
> word of vengeance: idle seeming.

> Meanwhile, just by luck determined,
> gods step lively where the flesh is
> and their progress and their concourse
> body feeds and mind refreshes.

*

Maybe it's didactic poetry we should attend to before anything else, especially since the various aberrations of instinct occur to me all too vividly at the moment; and since instinct cannot be exploited, pertaining, as it does, to the distinction of the organic from the human, of the realm of the imagination from the various influences and confluences of the divine, we might be wise to protect

45

ourselves equally against the detriments of over-indulgence.

> Leisure as the mother of wisdom, not study,
> scholarship trampled by truth underground,

> this makes a mockery of plans and cities,
> instinct of beauty while god was around.

The leisurely approach to beauty makes its justice most accessible to us, while it finds us most receptive, this justice, if we await the effects of beauty at our ease.

The effect explicitly of justice is methodically derived from beauty. We select our method and work it out from start to finish. The duration is predicted and one avoids a multiplicity of ends; only one end is necessary, in mind or in body, and the best method combines both in one.

The explicit goal, of course is the justice derived. Implicitly we categorize material available to us even as we see fit. The eye works freely, as the independent organ of sight. The heart comes into operation as the organ of thought and effectively attains, or retains, its freedom. Leisure and ease are of the essence, method is the rule:

> Tempter of women, vile prophet
>   asleep on cushions of moss,
> in love with perfection, striped
>   like a skunk in the soul
> but truly in love nevertheless
>   and the deer nibbles on your ear,
> which you dream into a message,
>   an offering of cold charity
> held at arm's length to attract
> the flies that settle on corruption.

In the house of mirrors called reason,
   though only by men like yourself,
the woods give birth to monsters
   and we all bow down to them
uttering eulogies to the soil and
   ready to break that bit of stick
on your behalf, because you insist
   on the cleanliness of the ritual
even though men's hearts break for joy
when you oblige them with temptation.

*

The particular method adopted for the sake of an instance of didactic poetry justifies itself automatically as the poetry proceeds. The heart must free itself voluntarily of any self-imposed burden, not so that it may fly, but so that it may assume the burden of justice and translate it into thought. This voluntary self-liberation suffices to endow the heart with the mastery of itself, so that is becomes capable of power, and then of powerful thought. The knowledge we gain on account of this thought establishes in us a fitness for the abundance of life, and any further knowledge we gain like that, through didactic art, poetry in our present case, increases our fitness.

Beauty surrounds us always and everywhere, both in nature and in reality, so that leisure and ease are recommended, even as an ascetic discipline if at first necessary. One lends one's being to it and comes away changed. Didactic poetry is in itself an achieved appreciation of beauty, but the achievement is not ours, we only take advantage of it.

That beauty exists in the way that it does
today and from now on is cause for reflection.

47

> We would take advantage of acts in the past
> or succumb like dolls to the brain's vivisection.

> One act especially may draw our attention,
> and everything else for that matter it seems.
> You have forgotten but I still remember
> due to clear daylight and visions and dreams.

The justice of beauty is historically determined. We have already documented its artistic derivation, poetically.

As soon as we take advantage of man's achievements in the past, the problematic aspect of time becomes, as it were, our working capital. We know that whatever takes time to happen has happened and if we want to make it happen again, imitation will be high on our list of theoretical preferences. Given that much, we realize that the beauty lies in the fact, inheres in the fact, that it is accomplished. Prior to its accomplishment no beauty was available there, and consequently one had to learn how to cope with a partial attraction, while the direction of one's endeavour could not be entirely just.

But now this beauty is impressive. Recognition of its impressiveness suffices to make us equal to the task of a beautiful work but for great beauty to be realized, its impressiveness must be infinitely sustained. The realization of great beauty comes under the heading of great art, in our case:

9. 'Great' poetry

The Somnambulist

> That he knows how to move without fear
> even where earth's terrors appear,

and he switches his eye on and off,
a human robot, this divine paramour

allows us to observe, at a cool distance,
with reasoned logic, how his flesh,
not tied to some primordial curse,
makes metaphor of universe.

Look how his head moves round
to absorb the physical sphere.
We actually envy his temper,
this tempter of the now and here.

His classical conceptions sustain
how he views love, or mountain ranges.
Even the earth his cool feet touch
thirsts for his sleep that estranges.

With each step he impregnates ground,
the dead clay becomes organic mass,
loam on the verge of growth,
green on threshold of grass.

His nature predicts environment
and creates itself within bounds.
But study the effect of his actions,
how he behaves, and on what grounds:

The sadness lingering where he brushes
some moss from a ledge,
the resistance of light to his gaze;

regret at the expression of hearts
cast before swine, or too soon
sacrificed to the mind's sensual swoon;

tricks of the trade called humanity:

exploration of life's organic workshop,
exploitation of the forthcoming rage –
then on to the second stage.

Hand to hand with devotion
to duty goes emotion of beauty and
this shocks the friends who confront him,
our victorious colossus, because,
as Newton would have it,
a push in a forceful direction
transmits, due to vector deflection,
the taste of god's absolute space,
unless of course man would equate
his electro-magnetic erection
with the security of the State,
in which case new particles pop up
devoid of indefinite articles.

Something snickers, malicious with glee,
squeezes eyes shut, makes sparks leap,
seeks shape in which to do dirt:
There are so many pressures!

Sleepwalker insists that if you get hurt,
you are not to be sorry for glory,
nor bow and scrape to a system called
world, hypnotically, by associates.

Sleepwalker allows the twist and the turn,
the jump out of the chair, the hair pulled,
but please do not intentionally upset
the neighbours, they lie in their sleep.

Sleepwalker dictates ignorance of
the odd crack in a roof tile,

the clever retort to the umpteenth power,
advises instead early to rise, late to bed,
the odd piece of hot coal into vain
corners of the brain, not too many steps backwards,
and fear not the grimace of the blue moon.

Over the hill, congratulating himself,
Sleepwalker's shadow snatches
blankets off campfires, calculates
according to code the savage
cloud linguistic, versed in statistic

tactile experience of foundation as prairie.

Oh the 'Green Mansions' of Brazil,
'Voss' in 'Australia, that mistaken German,
'And the Gold of their Bodies' on Hiva Oa:
Passion of exotic beauty become flesh!

(How am I to bear it? How do I bear it?)

Tom's joy ran over in the cave. And mine.

Do not look for explanations out there
where the critic will exhaust you to ashes,
that hateful skipper on your life's blood,
or you on someone else's blood, adrift,
waiting for astral light to shift
as spectral red, past solar mass,
then to forgive god his omissions.

Don't look out there, wasting the time;
extend the arm, open that fist,
rely on your Somnambulist.

Phenomena are in, appearances out.
Oh let the flesh in contentment doze

and don't aggravate the rose, the trusting
exfoliation of the erotic bloom!

Switch lights on in the living room.
Lie limp and wilted on the broadloom,
but only in some allegoric swoon,
the tired mind lifted, where its wrath
has struck the fish, has disembowelled
that tidal ghost, seated in female guise
near the estuary, no more gloating now.

Let cherry laurel cool your brow.
Everything may be taken up or left down,
freely, easy as that spiritual breeze
that never blames, but aims to please.

*

Here lie, in infinite disarray, her clothes,
she in whose splendid magnanimity arose
the care for small things, and no snake writhes
in her flesh, since her assumed body rises.

*

Sleepwalker stares at this in consternation.
He winks an eye, transfers weight from foot to foot,
scrapes off a cloud from heaven's blue shell,
tries to ignore, stares in embarrassment –
a flock of black birds courses through his breast,
streams through his head, he would melt if not
time's discipline had him rooted to the spot.

Up he glowers, whence shafts of light
slant towards that illuminated place
surrounded by nettle and red willow herb,

but he judges the occasion to be trite.
Runes have been rilled into the sand,
some building has gone on here years ago,
thousands of years – he clears the terrain,
he wants a place to sit. Deer leap startled
out of the undergrowth, a macaw shrieks,
distant thunder rolls, rain splatters down.

The lumbering giant cannot find
a place to sit, his legs will not bend
where one would expect them to bend.

Once more the naked buttocks are pressed
down against stone, then with a sigh
of mixed pain and relief his weight settles,
the earth reluctantly accepts the burden
but somehow still continues to spin.

This is the force of gravity he uses,
called instinct, fraught with rites and ruses.
Knowledge of that will mend his bruises
and slay the enemy he accuses.

His world is neither physical nor mental
                              but organic.
He sees himself as both continental and oceanic.
Behind the shutters drawn by sleep
                              for presentation
He knows one law, one force, one source of
                              information.

That the heart of matter is where beauty meets
makes sense to him, and that mass is a thirst
for beauty, the velocity of light an eye's
love-propelled glance: He understood this first.

That endless space shrouds the imagining mind
is his contentment. That the luminous spheres
cannot be grasped in simultaneous term
reassures him and he believes what appears.

Brain through his seated body enters earth
and down there taps happiness in bed rock,
dispels the granite's sorcery, the bone's pain.

For an eternity the swarthy hulk squats
rocking from side to side at times as though
meditating on some internal plan, stretching
the stiff neck till the vertebrae crack, waiting
in timeless exile, for the command to dance.

Flames shoot straight up through the solar plexus.
Then nothing again, for a time and half a time.
Nothing is felt but the disastrous deep,
pressures accumulate on the poised skull,
at times even breath neglects its skill.

So does the infinite man hold out
while elemental forces swing and sway,
break and unmake, corrode and cleanse,
geared to that purpose by the master
who walked the wave and stilled the storm.

Darkness moves in in droves,
pours through the eye in thick drifts,
locates an angel's customary station and
introduces fragrance of juniper and ice.

the picture shakes – the screen exists.

Surrounded by unearthly mists,
(incantations whispered into the dead ear)

Sleepwalker's entire body lists
to north and north-west so as to hear.

Out of the dark, in the dark,
the voice gives message, is message
which the darkness is, meaning this:
All who sleep now, if earth quake,
must either pass away or wake.

No more staring into darkness
waiting to be moved by spirits.
Take in hand the living forces,
know the god who moves within you.

Now is time for understanding,
no more waiting for a sign.
Rouse yourself and walk in daylight.
Search for knowledge that will wake you.

*

The mother of emotion is panic,
she of the rounded face and black eyes,
    face within face, dumb terror
pitched into the stream of ancient things.

She rattles at the gates of his senses,
    to be let in, fondled and inspected,
white sluggish bulk that would blot out
    the very sensitivity it creates.

Sleepwalker accepts the challenge,
not for what it is, whatever that is, but
    for what he takes it to be, and that
constitutes his first enlightened act.

He rises slowly, his legs spread,

we call this his imperial stance,
   it corresponds, duality outside,
to one unique organic stance within,

   that which is necessary in terms of being,
taproot into peril, through risk –
   then madness besets him from without.
Greatness can not be talked about.

   It tears him; would tear him down,
he shouts, flings stones at trees,
   observes himself, hates the spectacle,
sees what he hates, hates what he sees.

*

Man is reluctant to wake and stay,
but once the sun has risen for him,
   no matter what his aims once were,
that light no cloud can carry away.

   He flings the world back into eyes
that have not seen the light he knows
   and all men must be his enemies
until he feels that that light grows.

   One world would eventually house all men,
and really, if you think about it,
   it does so now, and if you are human
lift up your voice and sing and shout it.

* * *

10. Beauty as despair or laughter; self-expression

The eventual outcome of beauty is laughter, and this has to be explained in detail. We enclose ourselves entirely within the realm of phenomena for the purpose.

Laughter stems from an original capacity of the mind for harmony on its own account, irrespective of the body. Poetry capable of laughter is therefore not knowable by any particular sign. We produce it and there is an end to it: (Of course we cannot produce it to that end.)

> I am alone in my misery.
> Look, no one cares for me,
> even the birds peck crumbs
> from the street with greater joy –
>
> but my misery teaches me
> something that is unknown to birds,
> for I am flightless by nature
> and as the danger approaches
>
> it passes again, none too violent,
> me still alone here, carefree,
> locked into a prison of life,
> the key tucked away safely.

*

The reason we call such poetry laughter may or may not be obvious, but perhaps it would suit our purpose of explanation most rightly if we compared it to its opposite, the poetry of despair, where the body, by some original function of its own, manages its satisfaction irrespective of the mind:

57

Can you see what I see?
Winter has snapped the beech tree.
The lindens hang,
the willows crouch,
winter has not gone, oh

and the miracle of my muse
is shared out to the people.

Who can make fine
song of siskin in the pine?
Who can invoke
the mystic daylight in an eye
sacrificed for passers-by?

My own vision selects
singular pretexts for love.

There, borrow money from
gloomy tramps by the road.
Settle a score or two
but not too soon
for I cannot fill

my heart with spring water
from that parched hill.

But all the same
my body stretches
from root to programmed root
and its description fetches
perhaps a ringlet or an eye

to fasten my despair
to a lock of hair.

*

58

Beauty strikes the body alone as despair and the mind alone as laughter.

But comic or tragic, the devices fail us if we plan them, and this presents itself as a difficult lesson to learn, usually, which is why I should like to enter into them here, to the detriment of the contemporary artist perhaps, but for the gain of beauty, which affects us all:

> How can we make words speak
> and leap to the aid of the heart?
> Why should we not question the mind's
> right to a sustained effort?

> What we gain when we succeed in making
> room for another personal understanding,
> time for a new look at ourselves,
> tends to grow even in our absence.

> But we must feed on the eternal life
> as it introduces itself painfully
> and we must reinforce our commitments,
> if only by an act of the will.

The device used here may be called self-expression. Due to the presence of beauty as habit, the word is able to disport itself in time, and we record this activity dispassionately. Beauty is physically involved. The desire of the mind to enclose itself separately is rejected. Self-expression, as a device, could also be called a regulative principle, with respect to its task, but as such it would become the cumulative property of the artist, whose interest pertains not to art but to works of art, not to poetry but to poems. Of course this more correct application of the term artist is not in current usage. I intend to develop it here in a more logical direction , in contradistinction to the current misapplication of the term critic.

But the device of self-expression cannot be transferred out of context, or from one context to another, for this would hinder and mar the free devolvement of beauty. We do well to leave beauty to its own devices. That we recognize them when and wherever they occur is in our interest, as stimulants to profundity, aids to reflection, and the like. Their discussion as regulative principles will concern us elsewhere. Let us look at some more poetry now, and to the way in which beauty devises its own physical inhabitation:

Let a man steady himself against
the influx of an endless time.
Let him reach where no passion remains
untrained towards an impression of the eye,
and there he shall find the peace of mind
required for the attack on self-sufficiency,
on the original sin of financial strain,
which excuses his abuse of wife and children.

I too make mine an erroneous ambition
when from my mouth issue threats and curses.
Therefore I pray for a new appointment of
love in my soul, less old-fashioned an expression,
crude perhaps, if civilization were at stake
and man's best friend lifted a leg to it,
but the cruelty of my innocence converts none,
persuades no child to strength and riches.

*

60

11. Singular devices; sublimation, reflexion for example

Sublimation was used here as a device throughout. Reference was made constantly to a visual symbol of perfect beauty, in order to preserve a continuing presence in the sublime state, beyond the effects of the flesh, which were not judged, merely surpassed. Consequently the language moulded itself into that beautiful state. Beautiful effects, including justice, found their embodiment in language, and the device of sublimation, detected and then followed up, instigated the act. One would be justified in saying that beauty, which already exists, as power, desires to relate itself, to become actual, and it presents a device, which only needs to be found out and used in turn. So in this case sublime beauty ... but one should not go on too long about these things. Let us mainly remember that the tool we use is put into our hand for the duration and then given back. The particular function of a device pertains to a singular act of poetry:

> Staring out into a midnight sky
> I see galaxies leisurely floating by,
> more adept at music than my song,
> not influenced by ether-drag,
> the way these sentences proceed.

> And strange to see how on and on,
> unurged by elemental strain,
> in sweet familiarity with space,
> they put a stop to speculation,
> reminding me where my faith lies.

> The stars support no double meaning
> but they reside in clarity.

Their emptiness would teach us
our ambitions overreach us:
We have no business out in space.

The difference between size and size
is crucial, if not otherwise.
We keep our distance or we fall
into each other, while our senses
are drained of measure and dimension.

Our lips are pursed by words we speak,
the muscular contraction spills
the verbal seed, as love proceeds
to baptize universe and world,
acknowledging the womb it fills.

I pray that god may help us hate
the picturesque abstractions
devised, it seems, by church and state,
but more by my own muddled pate,
that would poison my actions.

Our holy duty to the dead
is to forgive them and forget,
not join them in some sphere beyond,
where zombies beckon for a crumb
and Dracula holds endless sway.

As citizens of earth and sky,
prepared for what the future holds
due to our knowledge of the past,
we must reject the Imperial State
in favour of the state that lasts.

And those who promise paradise
based on the politics of thought

should see the errors of their ways
before the judgment in their hearts
removes them from the present day.

The Artist meanwhile sits ensconced
in magic bonds of paraphrase
not certain in his heart of hearts
that he should judge or criticise
or woo the poplar refrain.

He stares into the starless night
and sees through everything on earth
and must invent existing things
to copy, so as to hold in awe
the disrespectful populace.

Myself, I linger in the shade
and document the signs of change
wrought by the wintering spirit's hand
for human kind both left and right,
tuned to the broadcast of the spheres.

*

Now the device here was simple reflexion. I think
this is the most basic device available because it allows
us to take advantage of that fundamental need of beauty to
be reflected.

With the device of reflexion we confirm and attest to
this need for reflection. This does not mean that we cannot directly reflect beauty. We can, but then we end up
with something else again. The use of a device at all, in
the way that I have been demonstrating, germane to each
instance of poetry (to each poem, artistically speaking)
and developing right along with it, allows us to lean more

towards an understanding of what we are doing, when the requirements of our own organic nature as writers or readers are for the time being not so crucial.

*

12. The beauty of feeling – the expression of feelings, liberated emotions: panic, timidity etc.

When they are crucial, we want nothing to do with devices, but we want to be able to feel our way forward. And whatever begins with feeling in art is bound to liberate our emotions.

When we feel beauty, therefore, we must prepare ourselves for an influx of emotion of the sort we must find unfamiliar. These will be emotions to be liberated. Their liberation, item by item, will proceed and succeed via the deliberations of our consciousness. While we remain conscious we may feel beauty, with respect to deliberate emotion, and eventually delivered emotions.

Our over-all attitude towards the emotions as such is bound to be affected here, and while we may harbour reservations as to the wisdom of translating emotion in any way at all, we shall have to make allowances for impulse and stimulus from the direction of our carnal being; never induced, provoked or in any way brought about, but accepted as luck or chance, as an occurrence with a statistical equivalence of one sort or another.

When we feel beauty we can then either express beauty, or else express what we feel due to having felt beauty. The former is recommended while the latter should be avoided. Let us see what happens with that in mind:

We alternate between the death,
the wanton death of needless strife
and mindlessness in wilderness,
a novel from of sacrifice.

We make our way through muddy streams
across the meadow's beaten track,
past groves inhabited by wolves
and suddenly we are thrown back

upon our past forsaken state,
when violets bloomed in vain in May
and tempted time drew vaguely nigh,
too centred in the passing day.

*

Another thing we can do well without is the expression of feelings. Feelings are how we feel about what we feel. The word 'counter-productive' was invented for feelings. But if they do crop up where we aren't looking we can notice this right away and use them up. If anyone should find it a problem to tell feelings and feeling apart let him momentarily withdraw the commitment of his mind. Feelings will reveal themselves in terms of distress, and this in turn may be eased out of existence. Feelings about beauty, when entertained, are pernicious and obnoxious. They train the imagination towards its own surcease.

With the surcease of the imagination comes an elaborate interest in matter, as 'Ersatz'. (I prefer to use this word because of the thing I am avoiding.) This elaborate interest in matter should be right away understood as symptomatic, as a signal to promote the rebirth of the imagination , but all too often it becomes self-serving, argumentative, and over-indulgent in partial concern.

Matter as 'Ersatz', as a consequence, involves the will and the intellect, directly or attractively, but either one or the other, since conscience, the unifying principle of creation, has accompanied the imagination on its way out.

What we get now, with an astonishing pertinacity, is a substitute picture of reality presented as reality itself. Since the so-called phenomena / appearances are always either wilful or intellectual, one invariably at the expense of the other, that which is presented as reality suffers eternally from an internal cleavage, a contradiction in turns, we might say, because as we look to the left, we see part of the right intruding, and as we look to the right, for an explanation, we see part of the left intruding. One gets the impression of being all the time close to the solution, but as one undertakes that exciting last step, yet another disorder occurs somewhere, which excites the aberrant faculties just enough to send them hot on the pursuit of yet another 'final solution':

> Do good like the mayfly as it spins
> vignettes of order into sun-drenched air
> or cling to some remnant of rationale
> as copper turns to gold in Vania's hair.
>
> Risk certitude, as melody climbs
> more profitably to an empty sky.
> Be anxious as rule crudely defines
> the Brownian movement of the firefly.
>
> I am not conscious of the world I feel,
> a world unconquered yet and ever,
> tenuous as the lacewing's molten soul,
> pigment and tissue, the mind's endeavour.

I am gone, fool and knave, gone
to separate the sheep and goats, the last
forces clinging to the earth's red crust,
an immense longing for the future past.

By the cold light of the imponderable stars
study the weaknesses of the man within you,
the perfect fish, the pretty fowl,
an exact image of the man within you.

Finally it helps us to rely on music,
music imposes order and the desire to live
and all the great connection love makes,
the demons extinguishes, the angels forgive.

*

The emotion liberated in this case was panic. But panic is so all-embracing, as mood, in temper, under impression, that we need to look for a precise distinction if we mean to recognize the area of experience where this took place. We should probably feel more comfortable with the notion of panic divided in a threefold manner. One of these would centre around cowardice, faint-heartedness, timidity, etc:

I am accustomed to remaining aloof
when in the silence only one flame flickers,
or behind the scene, where the sea lies calm
most days, a gleeful demon snickers,
trapped by the free inventions of mind.

My reality must be of another kind.
Neither the thunder of horses' hoofs
nor the blind fury of thwarted desire
shall press that demon to my heart
or make that lone flame burn higher.

The artist would say that the poem is evidence of the liberated emotion. But as soon as the artist were to comment on some alleged end result to this liberation he would behave reprehensibly and would find himself lauded as a critic, which hopefully would persuade him to retract. The liberated emotion cannot be tracked any further. Freedom pertains equally to us all, and individually to all parts and aspects of us, and it cannot be conceived independently of life any more than life can be imagined distinct from freedom.

A second division of panic would be an unknown fear, or, as the popular tongue so quaintly puts it, a fear of the unknown. We may go ahead then and feel beauty with respect to this fear, and we intend to do it in terms of poetry. We might also do it in terms of love or in terms of our conduct. The poetry affords us, among other things, an invaluable practice ground in the security of our own little room. Remember that consciousness is of the essence insofar as a deliberate emotion is concerned, of deliberation upon a decided emotion. Initially, we maintain, and with hopeful steadfastness, there must be an influx of emotion, as panic in our case. Once the particular emotion has been identified (not identified with!) deliberation upon it may commence (rather than a rash outpouring of it as a stream of semi-consciousness, or an unconscientious setting of it in trite forms).

There was no other way.
History has taught, we have accepted:
there was no other way.

68

Only one tactic remains:
the throttling in its cradle of
    all argument based on right.

And who gives such advice?
Who trembles before the thought of time
    as a personality with a clock face?

We should judge the man who
makes such a complaint and overrides
    the blind urge of fate with hindsight.

Oh, we should flay his back,
raise the price of his drink, dock his
    dole money to help support widows.

But wait a moment, picture to yourself
    people tied to posts, mouths
open in stunned agony, hoping death.

Make official inquiry into these deaths
    and nothing comes to light,
nothing worthwhile, only dignified pride.

Raise these shadows only, where the sloe
    blooms first to outshine winter's
crystal whiteness with petals of white.

Risk only the bitter thought of self-love,
    not trained to plough brown earth
but to wear shirts of that gainly colour.

Or look where the crocus bursts the crust
    and children learn to respect that
heathen strength, inward against bigotry.

*

69

In the third place then we come to that influential pertinence of the emotion panic which is most successfully summed up as an organic weakness. Not that we desire to make much of such a weakness in itself, once we have taken an honest cognizance of it. The strictest obedience to our understanding is what counts if we are to avoid the morbid patho-philanderings, or the craze for moral or biological purity, its counterpart, which laid waste to so many of our forefathers, whose heirs we cannot help being in this respect.

Every organic weakness has its counterpart, its 'objective correlative', in what we are pleased to call the world outside, and so it should never astonish us too much if we make contact, head over heels, with our own worst faults exemplified out there as symbols of popularity and collective admiration. Think of them as temptations if you must, as lures to remove you from the right road; but better yet to understand how our very reluctance, our downright unwillingness, to face up to our weaknesses as potentially profitable and advantageous traits, builds those idols and helps to maintain them. A careful understanding, and disciplined obedience to it, persuades us that even the initial attempt to escape from such an estimate can be turned to our benefit, while the prolonged effort to act as though no weakness existed, to behave as though it were only a matter of time before all such weaknesses are obviated; worst of all, to insist that the weakness is in itself a strength: this only impoverishes the present life and aggravates the disappointment to catastrophe.

The organic weakness pinpoints an opportunity, and it is up to us that the opportunity is taken. The relationship of beauty to our organic wellbeing could be discussed at length but first I want to give an indication of how poetry works with respect to this matter:

> Now all our ambitions have come to an end.
> The longing for the miracle,
> the green flame behind the white veil
> consuming love to the world's detriment,
> an endless rigour for the sake of a spasm:
> one ought to have known better, really.

> Oh silent threat to all that means humanity,
> overcoming you spares us the need for death.

In the interest of a more comprehensive understanding of what it means: to feel beauty, we might be smart to compare touching to feeling.

We know how we can bestir ourselves in the interest of anything at all, when it only matters that we want to do it and that we have sufficient reason to keep it up. So we may take such an interest in material beauty, for example, for the sole reason that matter resists. What we generally agree to call organic matter, which is the resistance of our organism, not to anything in particular, mind, may be 'touched by beauty' in such a way that the very resistance itself becomes attractive. What do we do now? We want to respect the attraction for what it's worth but we naturally have no intention to become part of the resistance ourselves, ending up as consumptive Romantics perhaps (I choose from an endless number of possibilities). So in spite of the theoretically particular make-up of our interest, there is beauty there, and we feel responsible, that is, able to respond. Due to our calling we may even feel accountable, in addition , for recognizing this

71

initial beauty and showing how it may be put to good use rather than wasted; or even made the scapegoat of a moralist doctrine that runs contrary to the organism.

*

13. Invention and fiction

The creative activity most suited and most suitable here is invention, and the thing we create by way of it is called fiction. So that particular material resistance, theoretically conceived, may become one with the beauty we find in contingency with it, practically received, we invent fiction.

The importance of invention and the value of fiction cannot be doubted with impunity, because the beauty rejected locks us into a theoretical device in which our senses cannot thrive but must perish, while the theoretical particularity, resisted again, gradually tends to undermine our leisure, to deny our pleasure and to negate our secure joy.

The invention of fiction begins with the fusing of contingencies:

> By a mile you overshoot the mark,
> oh splendid angel, whose wings,
> doubt and scepsis, beat the world
> softly into submission.
>
> I carry forward my plans
> even though none call me prosperous.

The result is emblematic. Let's try another example:

> Where do the geese go when high
> their cry takes human heart with it?
> How do the swans subject the sky?

A development would treat the emblematic as a phase
and supply us with a fable:

> There nothing enters me,
> here only the blood's endearments
> cast fortune to the winds.

> Kafka's horse leaves the room,
> peers in through the window pane:
> oh the terror of unspoiled dreams!

> – or indeed the matter of fact adventure,
> when doves exert their influence mightily,
> knowing your worth with cold, round gaze.

One aspect of the fabulous can then always be dis-
connected and drawn out separately, to create a kind of
chorus of consciousness, a flirtation with the exotic ele-
ments at our disposal at the time, so that the emblematic
and the fabulous are succeeded by the fantastic:

> Snow drifts past these eyes so old,
> mirror image, wishful shifting,
> hand to forehead in remembrance,
> and my harsh youth's panorama
> would exert the strength of lions
> on this present day's profusion:

> oil wells sinking into sea foam,
> robots trembling with excitement
> giving birth to slick minutiae,
> armies marching across tundra,
> steel birds pecking at the moon's eyes
> overfull with our earth's beauty.

Or, again, along similar lines:

The weakness I carry around with me,
like a stag its antlers,
to get stuck between the trees,
so that the hunter may find me,
unable to give him sport –
because he hungers for the chase,
longing for it most irrationally
as though his life depended on it –

this weakness provokes the gods of the cosmos
into showing their hand, passionately –

There I curse the historic fools
who make life difficult for me.
They shouldn't have altered the earth,
or settled on it in the first place
since their central ambitions were
to malign me out of countenance,
to steal my shoes, tear my coat,
perform circus acts behind my back
to steal my audience, tear my heart.

There I grind my soul into the dust
while an angry crowd complains.

Not a single opportunity shall be missed
to harness the heat produced by my brain,
the fever causing my limbs to be wretched.
I cannot guarantee a thing, though,
when it comes to kindness and a way with people.
Sometimes a face smiles at me, meaning:

> We both exist, but we
> both live in a hole,
> and I cannot agree with that.

I cannot agree with that because it goes
against my grain to describe my ignorance
accurately, my misery
correctly, the exact state of affairs
as though a picture of it merited attention.
Or a face freezes in front of me, meaning:

> We must bury the shame that would
> bloom in our faces – and
> I cannot agree with that either.

Are we not gifted with the capacity to feel
so as to map out the distance
                              between each other,
not in order to remove that distance
but to open the territory to habitation,
to travel from home to home,
for the exchange of this and that
so as to transform things into life?

By rote we learn to let life go,
by something some call faith
we say we like it so,
but oh, it makes the hard road harder
and exposes the isolated rock
to the wrath of wind and wave,

until the scent of lavender removes
the honest glow of marigold.
(No, there shall be no grave.)

Instead, stretched out on yellowing limb
of baobab,
from which the claws of tigress have removed
some bark,

I learn to listen for the sap booming
along the ancient arteries and veins,
and blink my eyes, hoping the breeze
will change,
perhaps to lament this day was spent
not within range
of greatness as the times prescribe.

Oh let me not tire, for I would feel
this space out to the end of space
where space becomes room,
and then let me lie down and sleep,
not from tiredness, but so as to complete
and be completed

yet again.

*

14. Understood beauty and science-fictional poetry

The knowledge we gain for the sake of understanding is called science, and we may understand beauty, if we put our mind to it. The effects of beauty, as we know, include those of justice, and from these is derived a proper relationship between mind and body, so that one is the other again, to which we refer as physical wellbeing.

Now one way that fiction can be applied in this matter, through the manner of invention, is by rendering it scientific. Science fiction in poetry opens doors for us where previously we were blind to the walls, that's it in a nutshell. I don't so much wish to point to a brand new capacity here but I would like to raise it to the level of responsible, technical awareness. Such an awareness may well be long overdue but that's no reason for ignoring it.

Feeling strives to be inventive. The feeling of beauty invents beautiful fiction. But of course beauty is its own reward and any attempt to understand this is bound to fail unless we love that which is beautiful. The willingness to do so puts us into a position where we become capable of differentiating between the beautiful and the not beautiful. (Not the ugly, since the separation of beautiful and ugly does not exist at this level.) The act of doing so, on the other hand, brings us eventually to a full understanding of what it means to enjoy beautiful effects and to have beautiful perceptions:

> Finally to lay aside all grudges,
> pluck out all ingrown embitterment
> because it drains the life away:
> That's a worthwhile ambition
> and I wish it came easier.

> Of course I want to belong with the nicest people
> and I want to continue to do as I see fit:
> One ought to go with the other, not contradict it.
> However I get pushed back into my little corner
> and for all I know that's best for me.

> Here I can celebrate in my own quiet way,
> and I do make available the fruits of my labours.
> The number of admirers is no measure of success
> but how far I can realize the values I admire;
> anything beyond that must remain gratuitous.

Invention and love do tend to contradict each other, and it requires a special effort to bring them into line. Where invention takes off on its own it becomes unnatural, sets up figments of the imagination in realistic guise, and these tax the emotions. Love on the other hand does require an object against which to train itself, or a subject worthy of its attention, so we do well to invent, but to invent for love, not out of love for invention. The beautiful invention is most worthy of love, because we can give ourselves to it heart and soul, so to speak, without fearing treachery or betrayal:

What a wonderful way of living a family is!
Not as an idea, mind, nor as an institution,
sanctioned by the Church or by the State,
no, I don't mean that. Let me explain.
More than one generation under one roof, for example,
and all that that entails: oh I know, I know!

But the family life offers so many opportunities.
Ask yourself seriously: Is it not the best we have?
At the moment nearly everybody in this house is sick
and we have to make a special effort.
We drag ourselves about, listless, disinterested,
and suddenly somebody develops a sense of humour.

Poetry in the household – what a suggestion!
But I think I know pretty well what I'm getting at.
I'm drawing on my experience as a father and a husband
and the way I see it would probably surprise you.
For instance, I don't have a single right to my name
and each day is a trip into unknown territory.

The children make a mess of the food on the table.
Granddad, the anchor man, smokes forty a day
and administrates the town from his rocking chair.
Mother keeps the home planned out and tidy,
father keeps the sails trimmed to the wind
and everybody is fond of Wodwo, the white mouse.

What a marvellous life we have as a family!
When somebody gets sick, somebody else gets worried.
Worry gets together with nag to make frustration
and suddenly it's a question of live or die,
but five heads and a mouse are better than one
so we can absorb a few more shocks.

Or the picnics we have, at Easter, during summer,
the weekends at the sea, whole dinners in the park,
everybody happy for hours at a time,
with the sun blazing down on our family,
saying this is it, why look further,
put down roots here, grow and flourish!

But of course one must derive one's notions
                              from somewhere,
one must speculate on the nature of one's fit
                              in the universe,
absorb the pattern, reflect the detail,
take account of every condition and circumstance,
(not bread alone) and the way we go about that
can cover us entirely, for all the years to come.

                    *

Or, to demonstrate the same, this time with more emphasis on beauty right from the start:

> My favourite love is like a rose,
> with bloom of white
> and scent of myrrh
> and sharp, sharp thorns;
>
> and I must seem like that to her.

79

How is it, she never spurns me,
nor holds bad thoughts
rudely against me,
and then her love burns me?

I must give this some careful thought.

If she knew how I feel sometimes
when it's dark in here
between the head and the heart,
would she try to understand

or would it cause her grief and fear?

My favourite love is like a rose,
with bloom of white
and scent of myrrh
and sharp, sharp thorns;
and I must seem like that to her.

The two of us make one life
rise up from earth,
come down from sky,
return to dust,

and we repeat that if we must.

We set ourselves this one goal:
to magnify
with every breath
the strength of love

even beyond the powers of death.

The reason she behaves so cruelly
is only this:
she knows, as I,
her heart's intent

and to that end her force is spent.

So when I gaze into her eyes
and she in mine,
we recognize,
as lovers should,

how subtle are the moods of love.

Or when at night she bids me stay
and wake with her
and brave the moon's
maddening light,

what works can keep my love away?

Her gentle though imperious smile
removes all doubt
and makes me sink
into deep sleep

afraid that I shall never wake.

But then I rise and am refreshed.
She sleeps a while,
removed from life,
yet in my mind

she keeps the peace my heart would find.

*

15. Concluding remarks; beauty's parameters

The way we make use, in poetry, of beauty, and of beautiful effects, directly or indirectly, defines for us the two parameters of our task, the 'left and right' of our poetic-creative act. What these two parameters explicitly are depends entirely, as has been documented to an appreciable extent, on the poem itself, on the poetry in action. The definition, however; the fact of the parameters as available material rather than as standards of copy, is due to beauty. For in the absence of beauty the duality of the act itself is discredited, while during the regression of beauty, as we remove ourselves from it for one reason or another, (though never a good one) the duality of the act becomes distasteful, regrettable, disappointing and so on. Hence also the recurrence of ugliness; not the absence of, nor even the opposite to, beauty but the sign of an opposition to beauty: a marked difference. Given such a sign, what is required is obviously an increased commitment to beauty:

> The training we do for love
> holds out to us the promised world.
>   Green spikes of daffodils
> seek atmosphere. The lengthening day
>   draws out green buds,
> collects the starlings in the crowns
>   of jubilant pines and then
> flings them into the air again.
>
>   The light that leads us out
> from self-infliction of despair
>   to gather us as one here,
> perpetual in the light of day,

leads out the sea foam too
that rides the waves towards pebbled shores,
    and draws the mist uphill
and urges the heart to drink its fill.

The two parameters here were simply the light and
light, or white light and reflected light.

Down came once more the blind
apocalypse and destroyed the mind,
left little else except a trembling
and the weak heart's dissembling.

This is my best relief
from loneliness and its grief,
from the knowledge that none can share
my own particular care.

And the taste of a death once tasted
repeats such a dull refrain
that sense and good will are wasted
and the stuff that makes pain.

Therefore I trouble the people
and impress myself on that scene
where sense falls and sinks
and moods turn into high-jinks.

Oh it becomes me to sit pretty,
a lucid fellow, tail erect,
not too proud to fail in things,
no face to protect.

But you overturn my world,
make a mockery of my plans
and dance away the time I earned,

refute the facts I learned.

I flee before history's onslaught,
the regression of everything matched,
torches held above swelled heads,
no strings attached.

I curse the makers of trials,
those magicians who hold life dear,
or anywhere my foot touches
I would drive out fear.

*

In this case the parameters were truth and appearance.
The appeal to one is followed by an appeal to the other.

16. Beauty and truth: the primitive parameters

The archetypal, or primitive, parameters of the poetic
act are, of course, truth and beauty, and every attempt to
understand this as an 'of course' will give rise to fruitful
activity:

But why should it be that the truth removes
repeatedly our entire stock in trade?
Is it to caution us, who like to depend
on derived existence, against skeletal strain?

Not we should die, but the seed implanted
in our flesh, so often like a cruel thorn,
and naturally one tends to identify
until the master comes and splits the brain
and growth moves from capacious cotyledons.

*

Imagine how those poor Greeks felt
when they emerged from that great horse
at night within the walls of Troy
and all around the world lay drunk
in aftermath of premature festivity.
Do you think they pitied those they slew?

One did hesitate, called it unfair fight.
They buried him in pieces that night.
Another, since he'd brought his sword to employ it,
butchered away and thought: I might as well enjoy it.

None of them were overcome,
the story goes, by the self-consciousness
that metaphor has been know to impose
on egos suffering from reincarnation.
If anyone felt sad, he hid it.
They had a job to do and did it.

I have a son to raise, and if he steals Helen
I'll make him give her back, because I respect
property rights in others. If he refuses
he can set up camp in prison if he chooses,
but I'll not pledge a nation to my error,
nor will I die for England no matter what.

But Paris was an artist. He knew better.
He had no need to follow the law to the letter
and this, to him, meant entering by the back.
The Trojans should have tied him in a sack.
And Helen? Well, how can you judge connivance!
That wooden horse was an Hellenic contrivance.

*

The desire not to stand forgotten
on some corner lot in the city
is a good one and should be respected.
Tell youth to listen to its pain
for there life's treasures lie buried.
The pain is pleasure crying out
to be found out and put to use.
Take for example this thirst for recognition,
for being pointed to and spoken about.
Would anyone in his right mind court the media?
Not you yourself is what wants out for showing
but everything you stand for and contain.
Because the parallel longing is spiritual sleep –
the unwillingness to be pushed out into freedom.
But then comes madness from the other side,
and circumstance contrives to send us spinning
like a loose rock down a wet hillside
until we become material in experimenting hands
devoid of human being, we, who should have known,
and knowing, counted. Oh stay far away
from the general mass of consuming popularity
only by arriving at personal decisions on your own
and doing it first, prior to praise or blame,
outside some trumped-up need for food and lodging
or the warmth of woman: security dearly bought.
Eventually all this comes by the way
and then you'll know the joy in a drink of water,
enough to share with the striking water workers
and five cupfuls over. Then the girl you love
can frown at you from her bed the live-long day,
you'll not need to dispute it. She'll ignore you
at her own peril, never mind, you stay put

and milk the childish anger as it arises.
Does that sound heartless? On the contrary.
If love can't reach beyond the opponent's viewpoint
it's likely greed and deserves to be condoned.
We all know what it's like to jump the gun,
to go off half cocked, striving for some spectacular
effect, to show that we can rule by magic.
But wait, my love, you only play the animal
to see if I can love by remote control,
independent of female wiles and whims and moods,
the very stuff that on more outward days
adds interest, wealth and colour. But look,
behave yourself, my love! Don't burn my book!

*

Don't ever make me say that I'm
not afraid, in a general way, like that,
because I'd be giving up the ghost,
and you, who can tell when I'm kidding,
would have to undertake some trial,
a channel swim, a conquered peak,
to prove that you can make me weak.

Like a mathematician in a cage,
you bear me a grudge, you lose
the will to coast when coasting works,
and afterwards, when someone looks
in your direction from that side,
friendly, though otherwise occupied,
you say you only came for the ride.

Meanwhile we spend holidays abroad,
studying foreign culinary arts,
but always preoccupied with reasons

for checking behind doors, under beds,
until it sickens us and we run
back home, where sense makes sense
and no one criticizes our laughter.

*

Now let me celebrate beauty's cause.

I watched, my arm linked into yours,
the children tasting time in the playground,
then they ate, in confidence of digestion,
not speculating, so far as I could see,
on some future distortion of their wits,
justifying that they now cram in
as much security as possible against sin.

We spoke to a teacher supervising there.
What makes them like that; so totally fearless,
so different from other children elsewhere,
not like myself, who trembled in school
for fear of being taken for a fool?
Is it some powder you add to their milk
or some doctrine to their unsuspecting minds?

Get down there, we were told; take part.
What makes you think you can stand and watch
as though your own life had no relation
to the sum total of the day's light?
These children play here for your sake
and they'll continue for a thousand years
in case that should put you in the notion.

Well, we tucked in our shirts and trotted home,
first along the embankment, where the blackberries
ripened and butterflies settled on blooms,
and we studied the inhabitants of a puddle.
Then we lay down in the sun and slept
for half an hour or so, then woke
and chased the starlings out of the ashes.

We've been doing that since, you and I,
in no great hurry to get back to the house
where Dolly keeps the supper hot for us;
she only ever sees you or me
in any case, never both of us,
so why not celebrate while we can
and leave the grief for when we're gone.

So spoke the voice of true responsibility
gained by a man become a child again,
angry in the first flush of his manhood
at so much strength refusing to be yoked
at so much pleasure going unprovoked
and the sickness, for a while, crept into his bones
and lay there idly, hatching vain schemes.

I don't blame anyone, but neither myself,
for the crazy plans my brain perpetrates.
I needed confidence, even at a lie's risk,
in order to hold out while death rode past
with his list of names as long as your arm
and I suppressed a chuckle, looked glum
so as not to draw attention to myself.

Of course it takes time to learn proper action,
leisure to invent the needful treat;
I had so many friends to teach me patience,
we founded clubs and joined societies;
Helen, do you remember, I brought you flowers
and you passed them on, to 'a worthier cause',
a calculation to turn justice into a habit.

First I learned to recognize the pain,
to assume its identity and give it a name:
heartless labours sufficient to put the sun out,
bloody transgression, a device to drown the moon,
and one thing always threatened to lead on
to the next without so much as a felt promise,
since warmth attracted but gentle corruption.

Then came the wisdom to decide the antidote:
even a bath in the past served its purpose.
The reluctance to open out towards a world
given to trumpeting the adolescent secrets
from summit rooftops shading the professions
goes into the building of a self-kept trust
while you and I meet on fairground and marketplace.

Born into the world I was open to beauty
even as I sit here now and remember,
and the way you showed me to approach beauty
speaks out now from the way I comport myself
so that here I am what I then admired
to the extent of my willingness to share with others
the bountiful nature: beauty's creation.

Beautify if you want to be beautiful:
hard fought-for contemporary wisdom.
Forgive imperfection by offering a remedy,
plant a new tree in the unpopular silence.
Make of your wife an object of beauty
when bare sensations crowd round for attention,
lest she become an objectionable thing.

Is it not good news that the power is ours
to make the earth shiny, like a set jewel,
to re-establish the heavens where they do us good,
to clear out the brain until thought from the heart
demonstrates a readiness to set up house there?
Drive a hard bargain but know what you mean,
even if nobody wants to shake your hand for it.

When exhaustion sets in, aim for contingency:
let the dog lie where the wheel threw it.
Make do with the grinning masks of people
who gather for the chorus while their leader takes a nap.
We all like a special meal on Sunday
and the lady at the chip shop uses too much lipstick,
so hold yourself in readiness, dancing bear.

Oh for the delicate contingency of the world,
the fibre of the bark, stripped off by the deer's teeth,
in the cold of winter, deep snow underfoot,
you break through the crust, nothing saves you,
in the pale light you lie and you stiffen,
never less yourself than now, under strain,
chained to the fruit of your spirit's disdain.

The pleasure we get from imagining our faces
hewn into stone, represented on an oak leaf
or turned fully into an ill-blowing wind,
should not persuade the contentious ego in us
of its indescribable, pompous beauty,
charged with all the subtleties of an aimless wit,
mixed, like feelings with no good reason.

Hitherto no one has worshipped here,
born aloft like a stone on a spring-fed fountain.
No one has dared rule with priest craft
of this sort, carried by the surface tension
of a world endlessly cloaked in beauty,
never too terrified to abstain from evil
though the ripe pomegranate deliciously fills the hand.

When beauty builds in my self its castle,
deep the foundations dug into bedrock
where years ago time stood still to contemplate
its faulty mansion and tore the walls down,
I stand perplexed, patient of knowledge
and feel my duty is not to ask questions
but to wait in readiness, in case I am wanted.

Make your home here, lord of the new world,
make this peaceful estate your domain too.
Often in past years did you send the surveyors
to mark such land as pleased you for settlement.
Forgive the impatient antics of one who
rushed out of ignorance into needless danger,
though all this is added on now as a bonus.

Of course we continue to make our presence felt,
but not any more in a homeless fashion,
depending on friction to cause the desired effect,
nor in doubtful association with human laws.
Only the perfect sense shares in our venture
and the happy, clear-eyed genius must reign
within this cradle, finally rocking.

Index of section headings: page

* * *

www.ingramcontent.com/pod-product-compliance
Lightning Source LLC
Chambersburg PA
CBHW060423290526
45791CB00002B/857